OCT   2013

HOW DOES IT FLY?
FIGHTER PLANE

BY MATT MULLINS

CHERRY LAKE
Publishing

Published in the United States of America by Cherry Lake Publishing
Ann Arbor, Michigan
www.cherrylakepublishing.com

Content Adviser: Jacob Zeiger, Production Support Engineer, the Boeing Company

LIBRARY OF CONGRESS CATALOGING-IN-PUBLICATION DATA
Mullins, Matt.
  How does it fly? fighter plane/by Matt Mullins.
    p. cm.—(Community connections)
  Includes bibliographical references and index.
  ISBN-13: 978-1-61080-066-2 (lib. bdg.)
  ISBN-10: 1-61080-066-4 (lib. bdg.)
  1. Fighter planes—Juvenile literature. I. Title. II. Series.
  UG1242.F5M855 2011
  623.74'64—dc22   2010051212

Cherry Lake Publishing would like to acknowledge the work of The Partnership for 21st Century Skills. Please visit *www.21stcenturyskills.org* for more information.

Printed in the United States of America
Corporate Graphics Inc.
July 2011
CLFA09

FIGHTER PLANE

CONTENTS

SUPERFAST FIGHTER PLANES

Maybe you have seen them on TV or at a big football game. A team of fighter planes, flying close together. The planes roll and dive together. The tips of their wings are very close! One mistake would be a disaster.

It takes a lot of practice and skill to fly close together.

Have you ever heard a big *BOOM!* when a plane flew overhead? This sound is made when a plane is flying faster than sound. The air cannot move out of the way. The plane begins to produce a **sonic boom**.

Most fighters are built to fly faster than sound. Fast fighters can fly into an area, attack, and escape quickly.

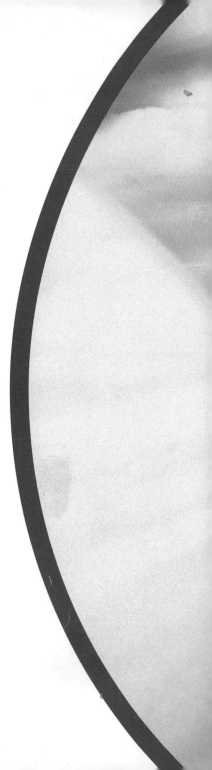

A cloud sometimes forms when a plane travels near the speed of sound.

Sonic booms are not one big bang. The sound lasts as long as the plane flies faster than sound. The sound follows along behind the plane. But you only hear the sound once. Can you guess why?

THE FIRST FIGHTER PLANES

Before fighters, less powerful planes were used to "scout" during a war. Pilots flew over enemies on the ground. They gathered information on where an enemy was located. Pilots carried guns so they could shoot at enemy planes. Eventually, larger guns were attached to the planes.

Scouting planes can get a wide view of enemy troops.

8

Most of the first fighters were biplanes. They had two levels of wings. Wings were usually made of wood covered in fabric.

Wings give planes **lift**. They keep planes in the air. A biplane's extra set of wings provides extra lift. Engines give planes **thrust**. Thrust pushes the plane forward through the air.

Wood gives the body and wings of this plane their shape.

At first, fighter planes had trouble with guns. Engines used **propellers** to push the plane forward. But the propeller was located near the gun. Pilots sometimes accidentally shot their own propellers!

In 1915, engineer Anthony Fokker developed a solution. He perfected a way for guns to avoid shooting the blades as the propellers turned.

Guns were mounted behind the propeller. A gun had to shoot at just the right time to not hit a blade.

THINK!

Planes made from wood were used well into World War II (1939–1945). Why do you think wood was preferred over metal for some airplanes? Can you think of advantages that wood has over metal?

13

A FIGHTER'S JOB

Fighter planes must often serve many roles. They are used in air-to-air combat. These fierce battles between two or more pilots are often called **dogfights**. Fighter planes also attack enemies on the ground.

Sometimes fighters take off or land on ships called carriers.

Today, guns are mounted on the wings or inside the plane. Fighters shoot **missiles**. They also drop bombs.

Fighters are expensive to build. Still, most militaries around the world have them. The most advanced fighter is the F-22. It is only used by the United States. It costs $150 million to make each F-22.

The F-22 is also called the Raptor.

LOOK!

Fighter planes have changed a lot since the old biplanes. Take a look at a modern fighter. What differences do you see? Do you see metal? Wood? How are the engines different?

17

TECHNOLOGY NOW AND IN THE FUTURE

Some of the most advanced fighters are not just fast. They are also very hard to spot on **radar**. These **stealth** fighters can hide from radar because of their shape. They are made of material that radar cannot detect.

The F-117 may look strange, but its angles help it hide from radar.

In the future, new kinds of engines may power planes at 10 times the speed of sound! New weapons may be able to hit enemy planes from great distances. Weapons such as **laser beams** don't require heavy metal bullets or missiles. Fighters will be lighter and able to fly faster and farther.

Can you see yourself in the pilot's seat of a fighter?

Planes called tankers are like gas stations in the air. They supply planes with extra fuel in the middle of flight. Ask a librarian to help you find out more about tankers. Try to learn the reasons why fighters need to refuel without landing.

GLOSSARY

dogfights (DAWG-fites) battles in the air between fighter planes

laser beams (LAY-zuhr BEEMZ) intense, thin rays of concentrated light

lift (LIFT) the upward force of flight

missiles (MISS-uhlz) weapons that are fired, thrown, or dropped, or that fly toward a target

propellers (proh-PEL-urz) fanlike sets of wing-shaped blades attached to an engine, used to add thrust

radar (RAY-dar) equipment that uses radio waves to determine the location and movement of objects

sonic boom (SAH-nihk BOOM) the sound made when an object is moving faster than the speed of sound

stealth (STELTH) intended to be almost invisible to radar

thrust (THRUHST) the forward force of flight

FIND OUT MORE

BOOKS

Abramson, Andra Serlin. *Fighter Planes Up Close*. New York City: Sterling Publishing, 2007.

Eason, Sarah. *How Does a Jet Plane Work?* New York City: Gareth Stevens Publishing, 2010.

WEB SITES

Kids.Net.Au Encyclopedia: Fighter Aircraft
encyclopedia.kids.net.au/page/fi/Fighter_aircraft
Discover history, information on fighter planes from around the world, and more.

NASA: Ultra-Efficient Engine Technology—Kid's Page
www.ueet.nasa.gov/StudentSite/
Find information about how planes fly and about the history of flight, play some games, and more.

INDEX

ABOUT THE AUTHOR

Matt Mullins lives near an airport in Madison, Wisconsin. Matt has a master's degree in the history of science and writes about all sorts of things—science, technology, business, academics, food, and more. He also writes and directs films and spends time with his son.

24